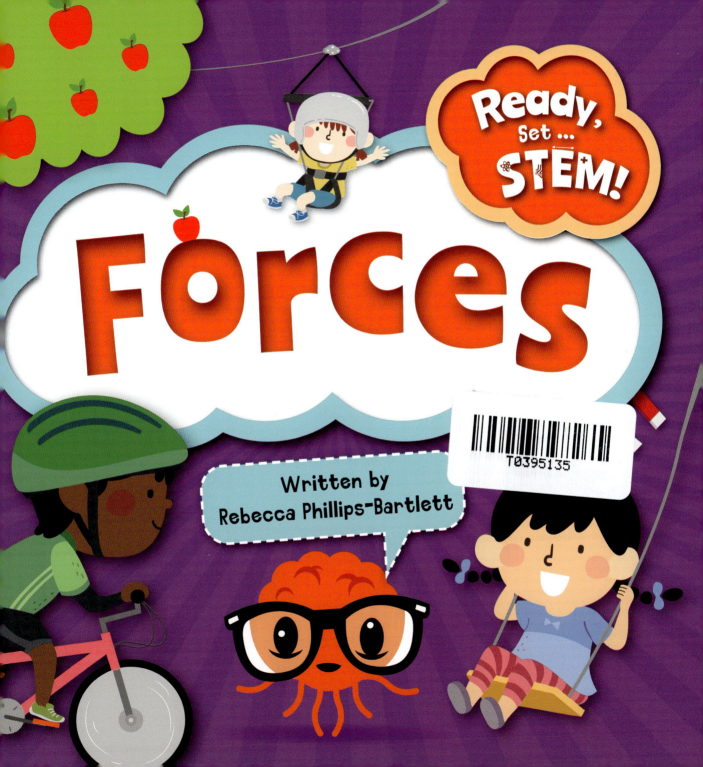

**Library of Congress Control Number:**
2024945310

**ISBN**
979-8-89359-290-0 (library bound)
979-8-89359-295-5 (paperback)
979-8-89359-304-4 (epub)
979-8-89359-300-6 (hosted ebook)

Printed in the United States of America
Mankato, MN

012025

**Written by:**
Rebecca Phillips-Bartlett
**Edited by:**
Noah Leatherland
**Designed by:**
Jasmine Pointer

All facts, statistics, web addresses and URLs in this book were verified as valid and accurate at time of writing. No responsibility for any changes to external websites or references can be accepted by either the author or publisher.

North American adaptation copyright © 2025 by North Star Editions, Mendota Heights, MN 55120. All rights reserved. No part of this book may be reproduced or utilized in any form or by any means without written permission from the publisher.
Forces © 2024 BookLife Publishing
This edition is published by arrangement with BookLife Publishing

sales@northstareditions.com | 888-417-0195

## Photo Credits

Images are courtesy of Shutterstock.com. With thanks to Getty Images, Thinkstock Photo, and iStockphoto.
Recurring images – Micra (brain, sunburst pattern), BNP Design Studio (children vectors), illustrator096 (clouds). Cover– BNP Design Studio, NeMaria, stockakia, 2–3 – GBearFotos, 4–5 – LightField Studios, Fotokostic, FamVeld, Iconic Bestiary, 6–7 – Sergey Novikov, SpicyTruffel, 8–9 – Q88, Nemanja Cosovic, Blueastro, 10–11 – wavebreakmedia, 12–13 – Volodymyr Voronov, vystekimages, Valentina Antuganova, BearFotos, 14–15 – Sergey Novikov, StockSmartStart, 16–17 – TinnaPong, 18–19 – frantic00, Inamiqu, 20–21 – Polina Valentina, Elena Platova, Igdeeva Alena, 22–23 – PPstock.

# Contents

| | |
|---|---|
| Page 4 | Forces Around Us |
| Page 6 | Push It |
| Page 8 | Pull It |
| Page 10 | Finding Balance |
| Page 12 | Twist It |
| Page 14 | Stretch It |
| Page 16 | Magnificent Magnets |
| Page 18 | Forces in Sports |
| Page 20 | A Picture of Power |
| Page 22 | Feel the Force |
| Page 24 | Glossary and Index |

Words that look like this can be found in the glossary on page 24.

# Forces Around Us

Hi, everyone! I'm Brain the brian. Oh no. That's not right. I'm Brian the brain. I always get that mixed up! Let's learn about forces together!

# Push It

A push is a force that moves an object away from something. If you wanted something to be farther away from you, you might push it.

6

# Pull It

A pull is a force that moves an object towards something. The heavier the object, the more force is needed to move it.

Pull is the <u>opposite</u> of push.

# Finding Balance

In a game of tug-of-war, each team pulls a rope in opposite directions. If both teams pull with the same amount of force, the rope will not move.

The rope does not move because the force is <u>balanced</u>. What do you think would happen if two people on the same team let go of the rope?

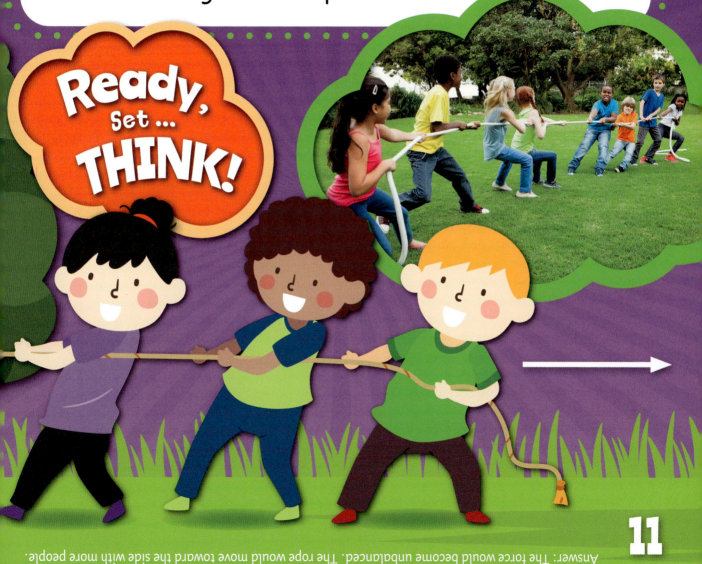

Answer: The force would become unbalanced. The rope would move toward the side with more people.

# Twist It

A twist is when you bend or turn something to move it. To open most bottles, you twist the lid.

Some objects can be twisted to change their shape.

If you need to reach something, you might twist your body around. You can twist and turn your body in many directions.

Ready, Set ... TWIST!

# Stretch It

Stretching something is one way of using force to change its shape. Some objects are more stretchy than others. Some things will break if you stretch them too much.

Bakers push, twist, and stretch dough to make bread.

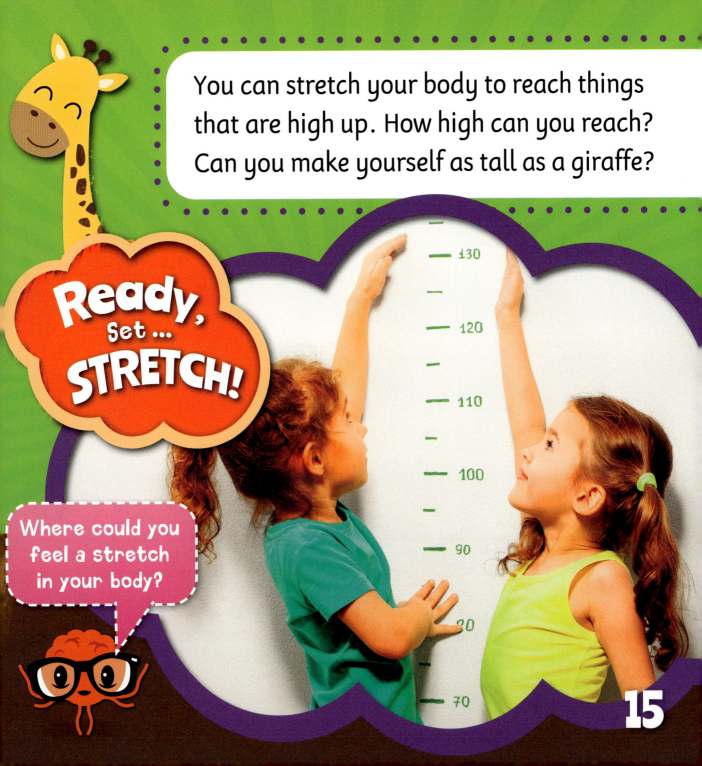

# Magnificent Magnets

Magnets are pieces of metal that can pull other pieces of metal. Something that can be moved using a magnet is called magnetic.

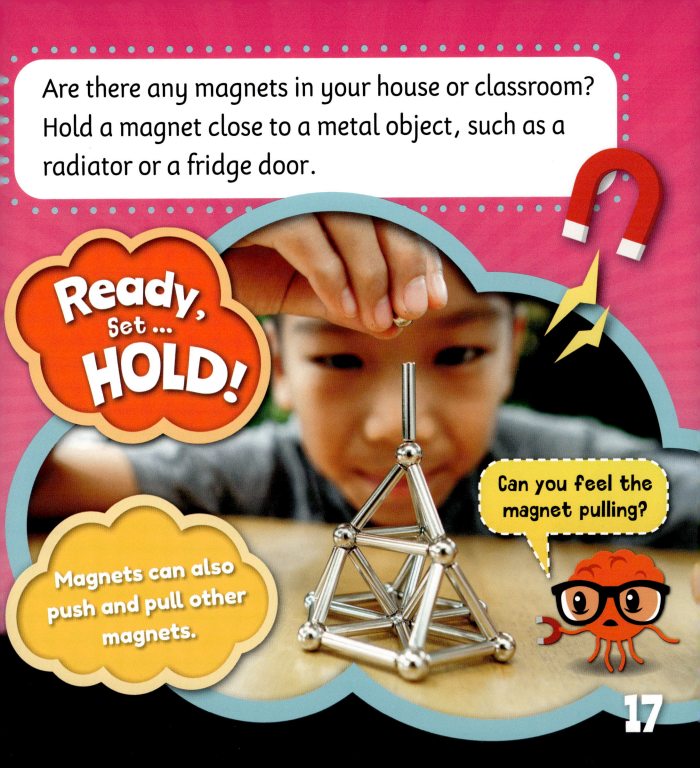

Are there any magnets in your house or classroom? Hold a magnet close to a metal object, such as a radiator or a fridge door.

**Ready, Set ... HOLD!**

Can you feel the magnet pulling?

Magnets can also push and pull other magnets.

# Forces in Sports

To kick a soccer ball, you push the ball with your foot. The goalie pushes the ball with their hand to stop it from going into the goal.

To jump on a trampoline, you use your legs and feet to push your body off the trampoline and into the air. What other sports use forces?

Ready, Set ... THINK!

Do you play any sports?

# A Picture of Power

What is the heaviest thing you think you could pull? Now think about the heaviest thing in the world. How strong would you have to be to pull that heavy thing?

# Feel the Force

Forces are all around us. We use forces for lots of things that we might not realize, such as opening doors, turning on lights, and even walking.

During the day, try to notice all the times you use a force. Keep track of each time you use a different type of force. Which type of force do you use the most?

Ready, Set... COUNT!

# Glossary

| | |
|---|---|
| **balanced** | the same or equal on each side |
| **direction** | the way that something is moving |
| **opposite** | completely different |
| **speed** | how fast something is moving |

# Index

balls, 18
bodies, 13, 15, 19
bottles, 12
dough, 14

giraffes, 15
ground, 5
metals, 16–17
teams, 10–11